T0146961

THE
Big Bluff

Veiled Evil Exposed ??

G. WILLIAM RYAN

authorHOUSE®

AuthorHouse™
1663 Liberty Drive
Bloomington, IN 47403
www.authorhouse.com
Phone: 1 (800) 839-8640

Published by AuthorHouse 09/18/2019

ISBN: 978-1-7283-2802-7 (sc)
ISBN: 978-1-7283-2800-3 (hc)
ISBN: 978-1-7283-2801-0 (e)

Library of Congress Control Number: 2019914486

Print information available on the last page.

Introduction

There are deep seated and serious conflicts happening in the world. The conflicts are leading to problems will cause wounds that may never be healed. The damage already done may, psychologically, take generations to heal. The next generation may not be able to cope with the confusion if we don't take a stand defining the reasons for the confusion and moral decay. Hiding the problems in a dark corner keeps us from solving the problem and pretending they don't exist is a form of insanity.

Political correctness does not help the situation. Exaggerated news puts priorities on social or politically biased issues where they don't belong while very important issues are given a second of recognition if at all. We keep trying to dismiss the causes because it might disturb a race or gender. Avoiding the issues will have serious and long lasting effects and will create mass division. Division not only among the genders specifically but among society. I think through the teachings of history we can find the reason for the problems. Finding the reasons for the problems will eventually allow a civil society to find the solutions.

In a nutshell, division creates conflict. The degree or magnitude of the conflict depends on the degree of division. Therefore, division, disagreement, and differences in any are create conflict. Some are easily recognized and a civil society will learn how to agree to disagree. To overlook or accept some differences. We need to learn to live with things we cannot change, else we will destroy each other.

History, as all men and women of knowledge and wisdom will agree has to be regarded as our greatest teacher. History will help us find the solutions if we don't dismiss it as old fashioned or outdated. Wisdom will help us to get back to a reasonable homogeneous if not synergistic society where reason and fact will once again reign supreme over hatred, fear, racism and chaos. All of the following disclosures written herein have and can be backed up by statistics. I have seen both sides of the statistics in the news media and in magazines for years but have never recorded them, nor made note of them. Largely because they change depending on who took the statistics and what point they wanted to make in their own favor.

Most assuredly, the news as well as the statistics and observations we make on a daily basis speak louder than any of the older statistics that we might have recorded.

The Bible is one of our best sources of history, especially when it comes to morality and civility. The Bible has story after story and gives many parables referring to the reason for the downfall of men and woman.

This degradation obviously creates problems not only in families and organizations. But in society. The basis for the problems can best be classified as spirits which seems to be contrary to a homogeneous or peaceful relationship. For example: The spirit of a lie, creates many many problems and is not at all gender specific. We will find in the cover of our Bibles that many spirits can be observed and recognized as age old spirits manifesting themselves in modern times. The Bible uses women mostly to reveal and disperse these spirits and men as the objects of torment to show the results of manifestation of the spirit.

The creation and solution to the problems can be displayed by the actions of women but they also can be unleashed in fury by both men and women. There are some things the male gender can do, and we will point them out but mostly at the end of the analysis of the problems.

This is a don't put it down book once you start on it so you will need to understand a few things prior to delving into some of the greatest mysteries we have to deal with as a society. All mankind is involved to some extent, but we have a basis for the problem that starts with evil in general.

Continue to remember, that history is our best teacher. In history we find not only the probable reasons for the problems, but also the solutions for the problems.

Clear your mind. In this analysis there is no racism. This covers Black, White, Yellow, Hispanic, German, American and any other nationality or color. But, it is most specifically about women. In fact, what we call racism can be attributed to any and all of the reasons for the problems. The subject group cannot be classified as to color or country. The minority we speak of are those perhaps one percent of the women in the world who are creating all the problem. Ninety nine percent of the women and a lot of men, are simply tempted to fall in line with the pied pipers of rebellion. Some women follow the noise and some don't. Perhaps this is where the reader becomes useful. The reader of either gender can attempt to identify this spirit and at the very least stay away from it and not be drawn into its web.

Our source of information is a much more historical and accurate account of the habits of men and women. The document is found in ninety percent of the households in the United States and in many hotels. It is the book most distributed book around the world. This book is not only found all over the world but in every language. This book of course is the Bible and is the foundation of morality for three of the major religions. The subject matter is the decay of society and the reasons for it. I suggest that if you question what you read here that you refer to your own Bible.

The Bible is the only historically documented truth we can find. In order to recognize many of the problems we may refer to them as a type of spirit. Ecclesiastes 1 – says: The thing that has been, it is that which shall be; and that which is done is that which shall be done: and there is no new thing under the sun. In other words, history repeats itself. There is nothing observed that hasn't been done already. That every action whether good or evil creates the same reaction. The problems and solutions are the same

Also remember that we are speaking of the minority of men and women who are trying to change the world to meet personal needs. These people care very little about what is to follow or who it might hurt or what destiny is changed. It's a true, self-serving, radical display of selfishness. The Bible, from Genesis to Revelation points out the "spirit" that has taken hold of many people. Follow the acts of these biblical women and the result of their wickedness. xxx

Bluff 1

Spirit of Eve (Wants to be Worshiped 8/20/19)

The Bible starts out by proclaiming, without a doubt that Eve, as the first woman on earth desired to be worshiped as God. The temptation was in Genesis 3-5, 'For God doth know that in the day ye eat thereof, then yours eyes shall be opened and ye shall be as Gods knowing good and evil." Eve was fully aware of God's instructions not to eat of that particular fruit. In the temptation to be God she rebelled against him and listened to the enemy of God. It wasn't enough that she brought sin and death on herself but she brought her husband Adam into it. At the time, Adam was just a naive husband trying to please his wife. We can just imagine the temptations she threw at him to get him to rebel against God. Remember her eyes were opened to the rebellion before Adams, so she had the insight and knowledge to know that she was leading her husband into rebellion against God. The same old things that have led men astray for centuries are still leading them astray today. Poor stupid men. The spirit of Eve is recognized and, can be observed in many women of today. The woman wants to be worshiped. In its worst form it wanted to be lifted above God. The trend is spreading. Being loved and cared for is not enough. Partnership with the mate is not enough. Only dominance and leadership is craved. I might add that she may or may not have the ability, the foresight or the intelligence to dominate or lead. Poor decisions will be hidden justified, lied about exaggerated or whatever it takes to make the poor decision appear to be correct. The proper or even a different approach to the problem may have diverted many future disasters. This is the spirit against God and any rules for which he stands.

Unless of course the Eve spirit can somehow twist the words of the Bible or the church or another poor soul to win them to her way of thinking She will have her way in the home and with anyone connected to her, or else. A little lie here and there does not bother her a bit and is simply a way of life. She desires to be God and her rules only are the only priority in her life. God's, men or the laws rules mean nothing to her. Actually the only rules observed are those that benefit her. God put a curse on Eve that she would be be in subjection to the man. This did not change in the New Testament. We will cover the scripture in a later chapter.

It would be humorous if not ridiculous that so many men fawn over the movie star goddesses that prance and dance and show skin and are oh so haughty taught. Some of the men are mesmerized. Stupefied like a deer in the headlights. The arm candy isn't sure what to do with the woman next to him. He is lost unless she nods to him the OK sign, or the go ahead or stop and glance. If we can believe the news media and the gossip, many of these women taking the spotlight today would have been stoned under the Old Testament law. I suppose a lot of the men are no better. The old saying birds of feather flock together fits the scene pretty well. I guess it's hard for most of us common men to understand how any man could be interested in marrying and having children and homes with someone who sleeps around and goes from bed to bed and falls in loves every week with someone new. Makes you wonder if they will ever stop doing it. Makes you wonder if Eve might have had a drug problem. I can just hear it. "See Adam, the apple didn't hurt, now, why don't you take a puff of this". She knows he will be easier to manipulate him if she can keep him stoned and in lust. He just keeps fighting the world thorns as long as he keeps her in roses. And then he will work, really, really hard to keep them both in drugs. She will probably be at home sleeping with the serpent while he is at work.

By the way, the curse has not been lifted. Men still work by the sweat of the brow and women still have pain in childbirth.

Kind of interesting to see "some" of the women lecturers on television, standing domineering over the audience of men. The men's wives have probably dragged them. Some lady evangelist and gospel singers wear skin tight Levis and or even sweat suits and even ties. They prance around and leap and flirt like burlesque queens. Some maybe couldn't make it as a Hollywood Goddess so the transfer to church goddess. They surely must have not read in the Bible where it says that women should not wear man like clothing or usurp authority over the man. Men should just get up and walk out. Let them scream and yell at the other women. It will do them both good. At least make them aware. Probably not change them for the better. Some already think they know more than God.

In conclusion concerning the EVE spirit, it is the desire to be lifted up, spotlighted, idolized, worshiped, and will do about anything in order to achieve the goal. The Eve spirit has no concern for the future of the world, her children or your children. It is a dangerous spirit and perhaps recognition of it might save your life and the life of those you love. Be wary of the association.

The Desire to be God is a spirit that has crept in at every level of society from the very poorest nations to the richest. Athens was known to have a temple where women were worshiped and statues were made of the great Goddess Diane. The temple was little more than a house of prostitution. Most goddess worship revolves around sex and prostitution. We can separate the two because they are not necessarily the same. But both sex and prostitution are used to gain the same thing. Worship.

Men are mere pawns in this attempt by women to be held on a pedestal. As always men must be made to feel inferior. One of the modern ways is to make the man feel he is inadequate sexually. Hence the sex enhancing drugs come into play. Probably one of the less needed drugs on the market today but being lauded as the only way to satisfy the goddess. Never mind the risk of high blood pressure, heart attacks and strokes and whatever other minor problems it might cause. As long as the goddess feels that she has control over the situation she is narcissistically happy. Maybe it's time for men to get reasonable and let a little vanity go. Of course the fear that she will go elsewhere for satisfaction is reasonable. I would remind you that if she is that kind of woman she is probably doing it anyway so it's time to get a little selfish, live longer and save some money and have some free time and get rid of the Eve. I don't suggest divorce, but I doubt if the Eve I am pointing out is married. She is waiting for the arm candy, or the worshiper to come around.

We have a little problem with the church teachings about Eve. It seems the henpecked Pastors and teachers of churches now are finding ways to blame Adam. Read your Bibles. The truth will empty a lot of churches. But then again, the truth may fill them back up.

Bluff 2

Spirit of Justification

Now some of the deceit we see can only be used as examples of what men can be led into because of their lust or desire to be with women. Certainly the desire for companionship and a helpmate started way back in the garden and the creator God approved of the lawful relationship. However, with only a few exceptions it is a spirit which is identifiable in woman that we can find the solutions to the problem...

For example: There was a well-respected and lawful man in the Bible called Judah. Judah's son had died and. Judah had given specific instructions his son's wife, called Tamar, to remain a widow until his other son was old enough to wed her. The reason had a lot to do with inheritance, and the family blood line which God has instructed them to follow. This generally meant a continued growth in the family and resulted in the care of widows, So Tamar obediently went to dwell in her own father's house. After Judah's wife died. He went to Timnath to shear his sheep. Timnath was pretty much a Philistine city. Pretty much like New York. About anything was available if you had the money to pay for it.

Tamar was tired of being a widow and desperately wanted to have children. It was a stigma not having a family. We find in her desperation that our heroin Tamar had disguised herself as a harlot for the purpose of tricking Judah into a sexual relationship.

He said, "go to I pray thee, let me come in to thee (for he knew not that it was his daughter in law) "And she told him what will you give me? He replied that he would pay her with a goat from his flock. She agreed but said she wanted a pledge for the payment and he pledged his signet and his staff. Seems like a rather pricey pledge and worth far more than a goat. Sometimes the pledge or promise that a man asked for favors are not nearly worth the favor. Later she conceived a child and returned to her widow's garments. When Judah sent a goat to pay for the favors she could not be found. Neither was there a harlot to be found in that place. After three months it was told Judah that Tamar was pregnant. Judah said to bring her to be burnt because she was unwed and an adulteress. When Tamar was brought to him she proved that it was his child be telling him what happened and showing him to pledges of his signet and staff she had received from him for sexual favors. She had twins, but Judah knew her no more. The act was one of adultery, fornication and deceit.

The spirit of justification was the foundation of the plan to carry out the deceit. The planned outcome, to her meant that one way or another she personally was going to win and be taken care of. It is an example of a very serious cause of the problems we have in the world today. Justification for ones actions to satisfy or gain one's own end at the expense of others is about as common place as the little white lie. Is this wide spread among some of the women of today.

One wonders if there had always been DNA testing if things would have turned out differently. The entrapment of men into marriage by pregnancy is a lot older than I am. All we have to do is turn on our day time television to programs like Maury and watch as the mother, or soon to be, tries to find the father of the child she has conceived, or to which she has given birth. One wonders as he sees the morals of women slipping away, if all is lost. Some of these women have to have several men tested in order to find the true father. Apparently sleeping with all of the suspected men within a period of a couple of weeks. We can't help but feel sorry for the man who is going to be obliged to such a promiscuous woman for so many years. Of course a real father will do the best he can to help his child grow and flourish. It does not mean he is obligated to the woman. Men should very definitely heed to histories lesson that justification for immoral acts have always been used by women to gain advantage of a situation. We also wonder if history teaches us that they have always been bad, or, if things are just coming into focus. Young men of today, if not careful in their choice for a helpmate can fall into a very dangerous pit. If a woman lies around and sleeps around with about anyone that is handy she is a dangerous person to have in your life. If she claims she is pregnant by you insist on a DNA test. Many times certain women just want someone to take care of them and the children.

We have many government and social agencies, (mostly run by women) who step in and provide housing and food for a single mother and her child. Thank goodness for these agencies. It is unlikely these agencies will help the young man. Our observation is that being trapped into this situation can ruin a man's life. These agencies will jail a man for nonsupport which keeps him from working so he can pay it. Else it takes so much of his paycheck that he can't afford a decent automobile and or the insurance which is required by law to drive it. In the meantime the woman is living in paid housing, getting food stamps, and has a free attorney at her disposal to harass the man at her whim. She frequently uses the attorney who is paid by the state. Observation is that the woman still habitually sleeps around and although, supposedly illegal, entertains or keeps other men as companions in the government (taxpayer) paid home. Free DNA testing should be given at the man's request to find if his obligation is legally binding. Jail should not be mandatory as a punishment for child support neglect. A reasonable deduction from his paycheck is necessary however to assist in the expense.

It takes two to tango. The male is always cast as the villain in an unwed pregnancy situation. The poor little unwed mother has support from numerous agencies and charitable organizations while the male who was trapped into the pregnancy is thrown to the wolves.

The problem starts at home with the Mother. If the mother sleeps around and acts like a floozy while putting emphasis on material things and physical relationship she can't expect her daughter to turn out any better. The pregnant 16 year old unwed daughter who is not really certain who the father is, more than likely has a mother who was pregnant at sixteen. It simply cannot be true that the mother wants her daughter to be caught in the same lifelong trap of poverty. Unhappiness and loneliness that she has experienced. I don't believe that to be the case. I don't know the answer to the reason it continues to happen. Why don't we just blame it on the male. That justifies the rest of the people who are taking part in the cover up, we can say that a familiar spirit which we will also cover is part of the problem.

Men walk in a sensitive area around some women and if at all possible should stay away from them. Careful scrutiny of their companions, past relationships are and the goals or motives that they seek is important

Bluff 3

Spirit of Accusation 8/20-/19

Men walk on dangerous ground around some women. If at all possible, men should be aware of the reputation and the dangers which these women seem to enjoy. If the spirit of accusation is coupled with a controlling spirit the spirit can be very dangerous. The spirit thrives in the female as the weaker sex because the male is stronger physically to ward off the accusations especially of sexual misconduct. If a man complained about it, other men just might make fun of him. Men need to stay away from exposure to the women who display this particular spirit. Careful scrutiny of their companions, past relationships and the goals or motives that they seek is important

A man called Joseph learned the hard way about a woman scorned. Maybe this spirit is connected to the Scorned Spirit. Hell hath no fury like a woman scorned. Joseph was a Godly man. He was raised to be highly moral and that adultery was so wicked that it was punishable by death. He was a handsome young man and as a result of his honesty and morality was hired to oversee a very important man's house. Let's put him in a modern day setting like perhaps the Gardner, or the pool boy for an estate, or maybe even an employee of someone who owns a business. It was in large part because of Joseph's morality that the owner of the house where he was employed was blessed. Unfortunately, the master's wife found him favorable. She cast her eyes upon him and said "Lie with me". She was obviously, an adulteress and obviously a slut. Maybe in today terms we lighten the term to cougar. We have a tendency in our modern society to think if we call sin a different name that in smooths over the fact that it simply is sin. It sounds like she made it a habit to prey on young men and in particular her husband's employees.

Joseph refused time after time, but she was relentless in her pursuit to turn a Godly man into an adulterer. For whatever reason, she desired to betray her husband and get her own wicked way. Angry and scorned she set up a trap. She caught him by his garments, tore one of them off of him and yelled rape. Yes, he molested me and forced me to have sex is also one of the favorite tricks learned by women for centuries. She was rejected and the spirit of rejection falls in to line with the scorned spirit. Joseph of course was put into prison. The scorned wife went unpunished. The good news is that Joseph finally got out of prison and went on to bigger and better accomplishments.

The cougars or older women who prey on the young have been around a long time. Back in the day it was more hush hush and some of the boys were considered lucky. It has come in to focus, now that social media and the news is prying deeper into some of the things taking place. Men were and still are very much at fault and to blame for shamefully leading the much younger or teenage women into forbidden situations. There is no justification of that. Even the fact that some girls are taught, by the mothers at a very early age that to get a man's attention or favor all you have to do is show some skin. Some grades in college, it was rumored, were obtained by sexual favors of both genders. Sometimes the girls go too far in the temptations or flirtations and don't know the borders.

Naive or lonely men have a difficult time in sorting it out. Men sadly fall into the skin trap whether the woman is fifteen or fifty.

The showing of skin involves everything from the crossing of the legs in a thigh high mini skirt to the, lowering of the neckline. These acts involves the majority of the female gender. Planned or unplanned and it's probably planned, is the way they draw attention. All men and women recognize this and to say that it isn't so reveals a certain amount of non-observation or lack of wisdom. The "flash" is a very intentional crossing of the legs to show as high on the thigh and even possibly the crotch. We see an obvious sexual pose even at the news desk where men set behind the desk and women sit on the edge of the desk so their legs can be displayed. It happens all the time if the interviewer is a woman and one being interviewed is the man. The woman is absolutely "shocked" if anyone would mention that it is intentional. The one being interviewed is most obviously either more important or more intelligent.

The purpose here is to gain an edge to distract or to equalize the situation. Most often it works. We seldom if ever see the flash if a woman is interviewing another woman. Very seldom do we see a fully clothed female rock star, or female cheerleader in slacks? The intention is to show as much skin as legally possible.

Legs. If you have a decent pair will be displayed at all times. They are displayed in weather so cold that men are wearing coats. Obviously displayed to draw the attention of men. Possibly away from other women.

Observations, even in shopping malls, is quite an interesting study in human behavior. The showing of the skin of the breast is interesting. Even very obese women who normally have large breast will cover everything else up but wear a neckline so low that it appears their breast will fall out. Of course it does draw attention away from the obesity but any glance at them will get the man a disproving look from the one who is doing the displaying. Why then display them so flagrantly. To the contrary, a women with small breast very rarely has a low neckline or even attempts to draw attention to her breast.

I think some of these younger women have turned to the nylon tights that will even show the mole on her butt. Of course this has nothing to do with exhibitionism. Just a fashion....

Some women and a few men are simply exhibitionist. They need to show and are not ashamed to show whatever they think is their best assets. This is all just a plan of seduction. To fall into this trap whether it's the teenage years or later in life can be a bitter experience. Time has no limit on the spirit of seduction which cries rape or molesting when and if the time is convenient for the seductress. We see it in the news every day that the guilty, or scorned, or the revenge seeker or the profit taker or the seeker of a moment of spotlight isn't crying rape. Repeating that a man has to learn to stay away from the woman who is trying to climb the business ladder or getting into politics. Women especially are climbing up the ladder by yelling rape or molestation. Accusation whether true or false has become a political tool. Men are generally used as the ladder to success whether the accusation of harassment or rape is true or false. All the man has to do to be accused of such a woman is to make a mistake in the signs she throws at him. The accusations against some of the men in politics and those business leaders are too long in coming. There should be a statutory limit on these accusations. When they are made, the men should not be afraid to stand up and say that she made advances to him that he simply misread. She made herself available at every opportunity flirted with him, and made sexual innuendos She made certain she could find times to be alone with him and hinted that if he helped her win, or climb the ladder, or help her in any way that she would be most grateful. There of course is no way that he should ever have taken those actions as serious.

We wonder if, as out hero Josephs problem is, that the woman after doing all these things, but was rejected is finally getting her revenge by crying molested.? Unless these accusations have eye witnesses and or proven.

The unfounded accusations as the result of losing the battle are becoming more frequent. That spirit has taken over where the enemy is losing the battle and has no place to go or no answers to give except to accuse.

The Racist accusation is being used to fan the flame of hatred and discontent. There is no real threat for racism in the United States. The culprits if we want to blame something are these things that we are pointing out in this book. It is upsetting to all of us to hear the term racist used for every decision made which someone of a different race doesn't agree with. To hear the accusation is getting. If guilty whether they are black, white, red, brown yellow, etc. etc. No matter if ninety five percent of his ethnic group agrees with it.

The spirit of accusation comes from way down. It comes from desperation, hurt, revenge, helplessness and ignorance because it does not have the correct answer. It is most definitely a spirit to stay away from and to contain.

Bluff 4

Spirit of Jealousy (Miriam)

Another example is used to explain some of the basic problems which undermine the political and family situations we have in our modern society. History always reveals the present. The Bible as the most historically accurate, the most truthful, factual and most agreed upon book of all time explains it to us perfectly.

We can go back to the time of Moses and find that even he had a little family problem. Typical sibling rivalry. Moses has a rather difficult job. He is God's chosen leader of about two million people. A small nation. The Bible says the group was stiff necked and rebellious most of the time. Moses has to lead them through the desert, with God's help of course, and provide them with food and water. If not for Moses God just might have left them to wander forever. Moses had a brother Aaron, and a sister Miriam. Aaron had been his spokesperson since Moses apparently has a speech impediment. He couldn't much leave Aaron to his own way, but at least after he messed up with the golden calf, at the mount where Moses got the Ten Commandments, he had remained reasonably loyal. After all, Aaron had seen this mighty man of God pull plagues down upon Egypt and was there at the parting of the red sea. He partook of the manna from heaven which came down for them to eat when they were out of food. His older sister Miriam, had also been a part of and observed these things. Now the Jealousy may have been there for a long time but it came out in the open when Moses married an Ethiopian woman. Mariam probably had some responsibility over the women as far as being Moses lieutenant in passing information on to them and giving them a certain amount of direction. Perhaps, politically, Miriam was concerned about losing authority perhaps she was jealous over the gap that was put between her and Moses. Perhaps a bit of hidden racism sparked the rebellion. There was a division in the leadership as a result of these spirits. After some turmoil in the camp Miriam and Aaron spoke against Moses... We can surmise that as the result of the spirit of jealousy, they proclaimed, "Hath the Lord spoken only by Moses? Hath he not spoken also by us"? The Lord heard this conversation and called a meeting at the tabernacle of the congregation with Moses. His brother Aaron, and his sister Miriam. The Lord was not happy about the planned attempt of undermining Moses authority. It is called usurping authority. The Lord said "hear my words: If there be a prophet among you, I the Lord will make myself known to him in a vision and will speak unto him in a dream. My servant Moses is not so. Who is faithful in all mine house. With him will I speak mouth to mouth, even apparently and not in dark speeches: and the similitude of the Lord shall he behold: wherefore then were ye not afraid to speak against my servant Moses. And the anger of the Lord was kindled against them and he departed. Miriam, as the instigator of the rebellion was struck with leprosy. She became white as snow as Aaron looked upon her. Aaron went to Moses and begged him to remove the curse. Moses being a man of God and forgiving ask that the curse be removed.

The lesson here is four fold. There is a very definite role that God has established in the church and in the family. In most circumstances it also applies to Government authority. One of the rules is that a man is the head of the house. The wife is not to usurp authority over the man. The woman is not to usurp authority in the congregation of the Lord. The man of God is not to be reproached and his authority in the church or the word he spreads questioned by a woman. Any questions or directions should be obtained by the man. There are dire consequences for those who create or undermine God's word and instructions.

We recognize this problem more in women than in men. Perhaps it is because of the weaker physical nature of women. Therefore, speech and or manipulation to gain ones end is the only way to feed this spirit. The desire for power, money and position is a temptation few women can resist if the door opens itself so she can enter this world of no return. Sexual favors or hints at favors and flirtation makes this a much easier world to enter for women. Men are more cautious of a relationship with other men but normally let their guard down when approached by a female. After all we trusted our mothers.

That world once entered, can be full of lies, deceit, greed, blasphemy, division, and fear. One lie or deception must create another to cover the last one. Families are destroyed by the greed caused in inheritance. Documents are sometimes counterfeited, the family is split up when sides are taken and the wishes of the deceased totally disregarded. Many times the consequences are not repairable. Stress and guilt create sickness and early death or worse.

The church is being ruined by the influx of people who want to change the word of God and the authority that God outlined in the Bible. The women lean toward fellowship and social activities while men can hold more to the true purpose of the church which is to convert and obey the great commission. While the tares grow with the wheat we can only use the discernment God gave us to realize they are not only there but to be able to ignore their request and attempts to deviate from God's plan. Without a doubt all churches are very thankful of the godly women who participate and work in the church. It is doubtful that many churches would survive if all women were to leave the church. Jesus Chris, the Son of God, was the greatest leader of all time and had women assist in his ministry. It is well to point out that one of these women had seven spirits (devils) cast out of her. No doubt those that we are mentioning. Her name was Mary Magdeline. It is noteworthy that people can change.

Let's take a closer look at the minority group which is creating the problem. Again explaining that minority has nothing to do with whether one is black or white.

It has nothing to do with Asian, African Spanish, or European decent. It has nothing to do with politics or religion. It involves that one percent of the women population who has the influence and control in all these areas to bring down the influence or power of men.

Moses got involved in politics in that as the leader of the people he had a challenger. The women who are running for political office today have no qualms about slandering the opponent. Especially if he is a man. Several political positions have been filled because the question of integrity of the male has been questioned. Most often the circumstances are highly exaggerated but just enough truth that it can't be called a lie. Sometimes it is a lie, but then the seed of doubt has been planted and it might as well been the truth. I think men voters are getting so used to this as a political agenda by women that they no longer pay any attention to it. It never ceases to amazes me that the media will take the word of known harlots or porn stars and give it the same weight as the word family men who have served their country of office for years without a blemish on record. It is obviously just to gain notoriety or fame on the part of the woman. It also amaze me that the media will publish the nonsense, even if it is a lie as long as it fits the stations political agenda. We very rarely see a man defame or slander the most deserving shameful woman even when her record is proven terrible as a liar or adulteress especially, a woman with family. No doubt, some women very much deserve to be exposed for the role they have played in some of the crooked political schemes. the spirit does raise a certain fear in men. The woman is just waiting for him to say something a little to her dislike. It may be that he is just trying to be nice, but is exaggerated into a pass or attempt at molesting. Unbelievable but true. Male leaders are walking on eggshells and have to especially careful if they have somehow upset or scorned the female followers. Women know this and use it to their political and social advantage. Shamefully.

It would be most interesting to see how many offices of authority were held in state and local governments by women who have obtained the position by devious means. Or perhaps used a type of sexual blackmail to get a position. We can see the deceit even at a small level when we go to the mall and approach a sales girl. It's rarely we see her with a wedding ring. When ask if she is married, she may reveal that she is married. The reason she doesn't wear the ring is because it would make it obvious she is married and can't use flirtation as a means of closing the sale. It goes all the way up to real estate agents and movie stars and politicians. Everyone is selling something. It is a way of life. Buying, selling bartering, and exchanging a product we don't need for something we do need.is just a way of life. Most cannot use sex as an opening or as a clincher to the sale. It would be interesting to know how many well-paying jobs were held by women who were chosen over better qualified men simply because the one who had the authority to hire was a woman. The subject one percent of women will not admit the fact that they need men. In our little story of Moses and Miriam. She wanted the authority and power but could not do the job without Aaron. They cannot function of get the job done well without them. I said done "well".

Women in their attempt to control have even taken over the spot of Sports casters on many local news programs. I have thought about this and come to the conclusion that the minority of these newscasters want the job so they can either be near men or want to be men. I think some cannot do the sport and as a result feel that by doing the interviewing they are participating as equally as the players and get a power surge as a result. Maybe some just impress the significant other in the male like work. I don't enjoy the female sportscaster who takes away from the sport and the players by the constant through body language or comments draws attention to herself. I turn this off and wait till the games highlights.

Bluff 5

Spirit of Betrayal

The list of identifiable spirits in history goes on. Again this particular spirit of betrayal uses a woman to illustrate the problem. It is a little terrifying to realize that so many of the destructive spirits are in the world but it is timely that they be revealed for what they are. There is the deadly spirit of betrayal observed between two warriors called Sisera and Barak. The woman caught in the middle so to speak was called Jael

This spirit of betrayal is lodged deep and once revealed only continues to get worse, until it becomes natural way of protecting oneself against anything that is unpleasant. A way to gain favor elsewhere or to stay on the winning side.

The woman Jael had promised her husband to give his friend Sisera shelter if he needed it as a result of losing the battle. Barak was winning the battle and when the woman Jael saw the warrior Sisera fleeing she, as instructed, offered him sanctuary in her tent. Her exact words were; (Judges 4) "Turn in my lord, turn in to me and fear not. When he came in she hid him and gave him nourishment. Her kindness lulled him into, as we see, a false sense of security. She was to stand guard for him at the door of the tent and warn him if the enemy approached the area. She surely must have had a change of heart, as the spirit of betrayal entered her heart. Perhaps the same spirit which entered Judas when he betrayed Jesus.

Displaying the fierceness of her betrayal both to her husband and her promise, "she took a nail of the tent, and took a hammer in her hand and went softly unto him and smote the nail into his temple, and fastened it into the ground, for he was fast asleep and weary. So he died.".

I just so happened that this turned out well for the good guy Barak. She went out to meet him and secured her own safety by showing him the dead Sisera with the nail in his head. She protected herself with little if any concern for her husband or her nation or her promise possibly even putting her husband and her own people in jeopardy.

This scene displays the fierceness of a betrayal of her husband and her own word. The spirit of betrayal of the spouse or significant other for one's own convenience is obvious as women flaunt themselves at their husband bosses or even their husbands known enemies in order to gain safety, recognition, or promotion for themselves. Betrayal against a spouse, is also a form of spiritual adultery. There is very little consideration on her part given to the long term outcome of the betrayal. The woman who by her actions brings her husband down in the community or at his work place by ridiculing him or displaying him as being less intelligent is hurting his chances of promotion and leadership. Some women who have had a degree of success, or so they think that, by flirting and or sleeping around she is helping the cause is sadly mistaken. The wise saying, "Behind every good man is a good woman" is true. Men absolutely respect a woman who is loyal to her husband and family. She has always been and always will be held in the highest regard. A bad woman has every intention of bringing a man down below her level whether he is a spouse, or even a son. They are interested only in themselves.

Subtle betrayal of the male or downgrading him publicly seems to be the new norm. How many times have we seen couples interviewed on television where the woman constantly butts into the conversation. Mostly, stupidly and off the subject or simply to repeat what has already been said. News programs are hard to watch when the woman newscaster constantly interrupts the conversation to draw attention to herself... Poor little thing.

Females must be writing every commercial on television. The commercials never fail, whenever possible to downgrade, a man, even very young men. They attempt to belittle or make fools out of them. I guess it's the only way they can feel better about themselves. It is seldom you see a pastor or Priest in a sitcom or movie that is represented as a Godly, caring, giving man. It is always as a buffoon, or a little immoral. It makes the rest of the cast look better.

These same women will betray God and country to obtain personal gratification or safety. We are sad when it is done in ignorance by both men and women. I am surprised at women who think they will find safety among the terrorist Islamic regimes by joining that religion. Islam does not hold women in high esteem and many of the "stars" or politicians who have sided with these organizations will discover they will be beheaded for most of the freedoms they now enjoy.

The invading forces of a county might discover that most men will stand and fight for their beliefs. A few of the effeminate men will betray God and country. It is possible that many women will trade affection for safety disregarding all other allegiances. It was said by some soldiers that the enemy's love cost a pair of nylons. The female members of a gang commonly change allegiance pending the outcome of a battle between strongest male leaders.

The betrayal of a woman by another women was once more common than today. Mostly it was jealous rivalry and we called it being catty. It took the form of gossip, which was mostly exaggerated to belittle a competitor in a love triangle or to gain a higher position in school or a club. It still goes on to some extent today but most of the target is toward the male gender. Always for the purpose of belittling the male so a female can wedge herself into a position or to take over a job normally held by a man. In such a case other females join the battle against the opposition and do whatever is necessary to make certain the female wins the rewards. When we say anything, we mean anything. There is then the OK now you owe me trend where we see the position used to fill other positions in the ranks with females as opposed to filling them with men with equal to or better qualifications. I think that a man must be very careful of this spirit. If he sees it displayed in a potential partner with any degree of regularity it best he find another way to amuse himself. Joking about a person's weakness in public or correcting them at every opportunity is a step toward more serious betrayal. A caring person dose those things in private. As a result both grow in affection and stature. I think maybe that if a man had a best friend for many years and finds all of a sudden that his best friend has been with his girlfriend or his wife he should cast aside the woman and resume his best friend status. I believe the woman can't stand the competition and will try to ruin the relationship. No doubt it didn't happen overnight and no doubt it was not his idea in the first place. She has planted the seed or he would not have responded. There is an honor among men that can only be divided intentionally by a woman. A man also has to be wary if the woman has accused the best friend. Make certain to hear his side. A woman scorned is known to lie and to try and separate the men so they don't find out the truth.

Big Bluff 6

Spirit of Adultery

We can't go further into the area of betrayal and spirit identification without mentioning Samson. (Judges 15) Samson had a problem when it came to the discernment of spirit of the opposite sex. Samson is well known as one of the strongest men who ever lived. His birth was the result of the prayers of a very Godly woman. Samson's strength was a gift from God but was given with certain conditions. He was not to touch anything dead, nor to drink strong drink and not to cut off his hair. Men of power tend to get a little vain and to forget where their gifts come from. All good gifts are from God. They thus think they can do about anything they want considering that they have the upper hand or advantage over their peers. His enemies were the Philistines and they hated and feared him. The Philistines were great oppressors of his people and Samson never missed an opportunity to give them a problem.

There is no doubt however as we read of his exploits that he had a weakness of the flesh. In other words, he lusted after women to the extent that it even concerned his parents. They were concerned because he found the worldly Philistine women more desirable than his own kind. The Philistine women had very few morals, if any and were not godlike in any sense of the word. To bring it to worldly terms, he found the skags, split tails and prostitutes more desirable than those of his own religion. The Israelite women had much higher morals and with very few exception would not have put up with the shenanigans of Samson.

Samson's travels took him to the Philistine city of Timnath. Here, discovered a painted up, tattooed, scantily dressed, easy on the eyes beauty and fell in love. Since the Bible does not name this vixen we will call it a timnite spirit. You can put Christmas wrapping on a pair of dirty socks and the packaging makes it appear expensive. Again his parents warned him against her but being young and vain he paid very little attention to these wise warnings. He of course wed this Philistine woman.

Now this type of woman (spirit) rarely falls in love with anyone for very long. No doubt a type of "groupy" due to Samson's strength and notoriety, she found it popular to be with Samson. She already has the love of her life. Herself. Certainly her loyalty to anyone else is short lived and easily swayed pending circumstances, peer pressure and politics. We will call it the timnite spirit of adultery. In this particular instance it is the spiritual adultery that is sufficient to steer a person away from an intended life of progress. There are so many like her that to name her specifically might have lead one to believe that she was unique in flesh and spirit. We leave out the specific name of many well-known modern women who fit into this category because people would focus on them instead of searching out those in their own midst who qualify. As we read on we may find that there are several, who would fit the description. Obviously in the town of Timnath there were hundreds who fit the description, but this one must have had the best bait. Actually and sadly if she were named specifically we would probably find a lot of modern women named after her. Especially stage names which would automatically conjure up the promise of promiscuity and love.

Women are supposed to be helpmates for the husband. The timnite spirit of adultery is a definite hinder mate. This story always reminded me of the farm boy who goes to Las Vegas and thinks because he gets a little attention from a woman he meets at the bar, and thinks she is in love with him. Unbelievably, men go to bars and meet this wonderful woman and are certain she is the woman they can take home to meet mother. Just a little insight and its free advice. You are not likely to meet the love of your life, a good wife and mother for your children in a bar or nightclub. Those are the Philistine camps.

Samson married this Philistine. At his wedding feast it was tradition he give the guests a riddle. He wagered no one could solve it. He had killed a lion with his bare hands and later found some honey bees had nested in it and had made some honey. He ate some of the honey and the riddle had to so with this act. No one could possibly guess the answer as Samson was the only one who knew it. Some of the guest, most being Philistines threatened Samson,' wife and family if she did not get the answer to the riddle from Samson. Her coaxing and crying and nagging went on their whole honeymoon. She should have trusted her husband to protect her and her family. He was the strongest man in the world. What a way to spend your honeymoon. He should have also been able to trust his bride. Proverbs 25-24, It is better to dwell in the corner of a housetop than with a brawling woman in a large house. After seven days of nagging he finally broke down and gave her the answer. Samson's enemies of course asked her to reveal the answer to the riddle. Wanting to please others and appear oh so knowledgeable of course she told them. H"out of the eater came forth meat and out of the strong came forth sweetness. wife betrayed him revealing the answer to a riddle he had posed to the party guest.

He had given her the answer in confidence. She revealed the answer to the other men who were present. There had been a wager placed that no one could guess the answer. His wife's betrayal of his confidence was "spiritual adultery". He lost quite a bit of money and it was quite embarrassing for his wife to betray him on his wedding night. He chastised the men by saying that it was not right that they should lay with his heifer. Kind of a cute saying. I hope it catches on. There doesn't seem to be many morals now when it comes to laying with another man's heifer. Of course the heifers have to oblige and there seems to be a few around who are more than willing. Embarrassing to the husband or boyfriend I would think. I hope so. Can't blame the poor little timnite spirit led woman. There are so many strong men and athletes and they are so persuasive.

You can take the boy out of the country but you can't take the country out of the boy. Easy marks for the timnite spirit. Samson took revenge on them by burning all their clothes and their fields. The Philistines always hated him but now revenge and murder was on their minds.

The Timnath woman no doubt, simply put on a little more paint, and showed a little more skin and waited for the next conquest. This spirit will rebel against her husband in about anything he tries to do if it conflicts with her own interest or status. It is spiritual adultery in its worst form. This spirit feels that her guidance, input and popularity is more important and will belittle her husband if necessary to appear above and to get her way. One of the most miserable choices for a mate. Oddly we see this spirit in TV and movies where the husband or companion as an awkward, stumbling bumbling fool. He is often portrayed as so slow minded he has to be prompted as to what he should eat or wear. Interjecting, it is hilarious to see how some of the women dress the husbands or boyfriend on vacation. He wears a matching outfit with white shoes and belt, a pair of poor fitting Bermuda shorts and a pink shirt. The media would have you to believe that even the timnite girls are smarter and more capable of making the decisions for running the household and spending the money than the husband. Of course they don't make the money they are just more capable of spending. Women never seem to miss the opportunity to belittle the male members of our society.

The political situation is a ruthless arena where women are almost totally unchallenged concerning verbal abuse and slander. Betrayal of confidence is apparent if the political agenda don't match or can't be agreed on. I remember a politician who misspelled potato one time. All hell broke loose because he happened to be of an opposing political party of the Hollywood crowd and at displayed decent morals. One by one and relentlessly the lifted themselves up by ridiculing repeating this simple mistake. They probably didn't know how to spell it themselves until someone told them. While lifting themselves up they put a blite on the reputation of a very good man. No doubt his family suffered as well. The media could have cared less. It's the timnite spirit of betrayal and spiritual adultery. The timnite spirit will betray anyone to get into the spotlight. Betray confidences to get the five minutes of fame and to stand out in the group. This spirit has very little worth to give. She can only act out a heroine's life. It can only be brave and hones and helpful on screen and while reading a script. It's a little like cosmetics on your personality. Forgetting who you really are by pretending to be someone else. Any woman who constantly degrades or belittle men or male authority should not be a part of a male fellowship or a group gathering. The do not belong on boards of directors or groups where nonpartisan or decisions concerning direction have to be made. A man married to this spirit will eventually after a period of degradation and belittlement will become the non-thinking, unaware pawn that she intended. He will not be thought well of among men or women. This is of course the timnite spirits intention. Whether it be politically motivated, or to obtain dominance in the group or the organization or the home.

Gossip is simply another form of betrayal. A confidence spread as the result of betrayal usually growing in dimension and accuracy each time the tale is told.

Bluff 7

Spirit of Whoredom

Samson, is an excellent lesson for what men should "not" do in the search for a helpmate. As stated previously the package does not always represent what is inside. The Philistines were now on the warpath and planned to kill Samson. It was not going to be easy. His super strength was well known and these men were mostly cowards. Cowards and weak men and scorned women always plan a trap of some kind in order to dispose of a man. Not having learned his lesson, he met another woman whose name was Delilah. Once the Philistines saw that our hero was once again considering the bait, they reacted swiftly and contacted Delilah.

Delilah was on the take from the beginning and there was no doubt in any one's eyes, but Samson; that gold, silver and riches were her gods. Delilah, being a Philistine also, and perhaps an experienced harlot told

Samson that he was the only one. Of course his ego believed it. I think most men would like to feel, and are made to believe that they are the only one. And they probably are, until someone else comes around who may have a little more money, or notoriety. I once heard it said that women get married so they can look honorable until they actually find the husband they want. Could be true. We hope not, but it seems a few married women are still looking.

As I said, Delilah being a Philistine and a harlot, was approachable and game for about anything that paid a few dollars and got her some attention. The King of the Philistines figured it was an easy way to set a trap to find out the source of Samson;s strength in order to kill him. The plot was hatched and the trap baited. The easiest way to trap a man is to use a woman as bait. Delilah was eager to be the bait. Samson walked into the trap with his eyes open and we question whether he would take a bite of the apple. Did he learn anything from past experiences. Did Samson heed his parent's warnings? Would Samson take a bite of the apple? We should pay closer attention to history. The mistakes we make as well as the mistakes of others. Life would go a lot better for us.

We learn that he indeed had learned his lesson and fought valiantly to keep the secret of his strength from Delilah. She would coo and kiss and request that he tell her the secrets. He would hint at the sources but didn't reveal the truth to her. Each time he told her she would run and tell the captain of the Philistines and they would come to kill him. But each time he fought them off. The nagging was relentless. By this time Samson has broken the second vow he had drunk strong drink. The nagging had driven him to drink. Three strikes and you're out. When it was discovered after several times that he had not told her the secret, she changed her approach. She went into the most deadly deceitful method of extrapolating information. She cried and ask forgiveness. She went back into his arms. What an idiot and what a nagging woman. She just would not give up. Finally she started saying the things that historically work. Things like if you loved me you would tell me the secret, and I promise I will not do it again and probably you know I love only you Samson. Probably a little crying or sniffing while all perfumed up and showing as much skin as needed. You know. The normal and historical weapons. Samson finally yielded and told her that if his hair was cut he would lose his strength. He bit the apple.

So you can guess what happened next. As soon as she wore him down with sex, booze and or drugs, she cut off his hair. Sometimes we wonder about Samson. He apparently thought he could trust and handle a nagging, harlot, gold digger. After she cut off his hair she called out the philistine drug dealer, pimps and God haters and of course they easily bound, gaffed and put out the eyes of the strongest man who ever lived.

The spirit displayed by Delilah displays one of the many spirits that are controlling a large percent of the world. One wonders if this spirit is handed down through the DNA. Delilah nagged and manipulated a man until she simply wore him down. No doubt sometimes playfully and at times aggressive and mean spirited but nonetheless effective with the same goal and purpose. Defeat and disable the man. No man can withstand the constant running off of the mouth, accusations, lies, belittlement, and emasculation for very long. If not beautiful, the best weapon a woman has is her mouth. Together they can be devastating. The tongue is a most deadly weapon that cannot be tamed. This secret weapon has been handed down from mother to daughter. The nagging and noise to most men is almost intolerable. It is a noise and an irritant that cannot be stopped by reason, logic or kindness. Men usually combat this evil in one of several ways. Weak or trapped men give in to it and let her have her way. Some escape to a bar or drugs. This pleases the woman because it makes him easier to handle in a drugged or drunken condition. Some escape to another woman. In this case he is just going from the frying pan into the fire. Some women get into a man's face so bad that he can't fight back verbally and sometimes results to violence just to shut her up. That is why we see domestic violence. The verbal abuse to some men is worse than physical abuse. Some of the experts say a man should never hit a woman under any circumstances. The experts have apparently never been on the receiving end of screaming, out of control, raged accusing female who's is swinging at you with every intent to kill. I think some women drive a man to strike her. It always gives her the upper hand with the law, in divorce court and with the children. Or for that matter anyone else she can go running to show them a bruise or to show how her mean old husband abused her just because she tried to stab him. Much of the time it gives her the excuse to run to the arms of her lover. I have wandered how many of these lover s are other women.

Maybe the experts are right. Never hit a women. First of all it will never solve the problem and only aggravate the situation. Just leave her if she doesn't shut up. If it is her fault she more than likely has only once chance of changing. If it's the man's fault then change, but don't find solace in alcohol or drugs. Don't worry about the kids. Sooner or later she will verbally abuse them as well and they too will leave.

I know this sounds harsh, but reminding you once again we are talking about a very small minority of women. The problem is some of them have the ears of a great many women. This minority is of every color and nationality but we can classify many of them as Philistines. These women are setting standard, examples, writing laws, and doing what they can to ruin men of today.

The rewards are there but not that great. Certainly many strive for the monetary rewards and in most cases they are assured. But it can't be the only reason. We can tell from the interviews of some of these women that there is a definite hatred of the male gender and the perceived if not exaggerated dominion that they have over them. It's pretty much been documented that prostitutes hate men. Recognition and gaining the spotlight an obvious reason. If not for money and spotlight why else would a woman go back several years to point out to the whole world something that someone supposedly done to them.? I propose that is only the alpha male that the woman wants to bring down. The man in control, the decision maker, the boss, the leader. Perhaps she desires to be a man. Delilah thought, no doubt, as the result of capturing Samson, she was something great. She was invited to all the parties, admired and was obviously rich as the result of the gold she had acquired by the emasculation of Samson. She was even invited to the party to celebrate his torture and death. It was at that celebration that Samson's eyes were opened and he saw long enough to bring the pillars down which hold up the roof. The roof collapse killing her and all that were present. As men's eyes are opened the roof is getting ready to collapse on some of the women. As men start realizing the treachery that lies under that beautiful skin. The treachery that lies under the garments of royalty. This book will never change the Delilahs. It may make them more careful. Hopefully it will allow good men to recognize the manipulation and deceit that that a few women are capable of masterminding.

History speaks for itself. To make it appear that all women are like Delilah would imply that all men are like Samson. That is no the intention. But, to say that there are no such women like her would be naive.

Bluff 8

Spirit Witchcraft of Jezebel:

Obviously this is a specific analysis of part of the cause for the problems we observe. Some of this sounds pretty rough, but consider that it hopefully identifies the underlying spirit of only about a tenth of one percent of the women in the world. No doubt that the majority of men and women establish the various positions of leadership and are promoted and respected for the work they do and positions they hold. We can identify some of the havoc and chaos we observe in the world and especially the division created with the Jezebel spirit. It is the spirit of witchcraft.

Jezebel was a woman who was so evil, that the Bible uses her to define evil. She was a politician of sorts and a witch by trade.

Witchcraft is probably the fastest growing religion in the world. It is the ungodly women's choice of a religion. It has permeated every society and as well as every religion. I prophesied of a witch like woman in my book "Signs and Wonders". She is still around and has many followers. A witch can no longer be identified as having long noses and riding brooms. They are just as likely to be beauty queens riding in limousines or grandmas on the bus. More than likely they are nice looking women, who drive nice cars, and are very articulate. Charm and lies are there biggest weapons. Men witches are called warlocks. There king is the father of lies.

Queen Jezebel was married to a King Ahab. He was not a very smart King. She used his Kingship of course as a way to get what she wanted under the guise of getting it for the King.

As usual it was also about the kingdom and what she felt was best for it. She was under a deluded impression that what was best for her was also best for the kingdom and all of its subjects. She was very good at politics. As usual, those women who are good at politics are generally good at speaking. We know by history that although the tongue is a small part of the body it can kindle or create great strife. The tongue can no man tame and it is an unruly evil full of deadly poison. For many women, and surely for every witch, it is the weapon of choice. The tongue can be used in secret, and can tear down in five minutes a good reputation that has taken years to build. The victim of the gossip may never know the reason for his problems or who created the gossip. The problem is what was said about him may or may not be true. Most often, it is either a misunderstanding, exaggerated or simply a lie.

Jezebel charmed even the enemies of the King to start rumors against Naboth a poor farmer. King Ahab wanted the poor farmer's garden. The garden was an inheritance and the farmer wanted to keep it. It didn't upset the King as much as it did Jezebel. She tried to buy the land and Naboth did not want to sell it so Jezebel started rumors that he was a hypocrite, a blasphemer, and adulterer and probably every other bad thing she could think of to get him killed. The men who worshiped the god Belial bore witness against Naboth. The woman Jezebel was a woman who might have been dressed in royal garb. She probably smelled good and looked good. Jezebel, no doubt, was much adorned in jewelry and make up to the extent that the true Jezebel could not be discerned. Probably many of the Kings Advisors and court feared her because she had the Kings ear constantly. Forgery and deceit to Jezebel was just another way of manipulation. She was not hesitate to forge the Kings name and did so to bring down her personal enemies. She was a very stately and regal Queen in all appearance. On the Inside however she was a witch, pure filth, dark and dirty. It seems the political arena is a favorite place for evil to rest. Witches like to have political power. They surround themselves with other witches and sacrifice children under the guise of helping them. They propose they know better how to raise your daughters than the mothers. They sacrifice babies through abortion.

There was no truth in Jezebel. She especially hated prophets (men of God), and killed as many as she had the opportunity. Godly men expose evil. Evil does not like to be exposed. It appears that manipulation through gossip and accusation has been the witch's trait down through the ages. For some reason there are a few women who have no fear of changing circumstances to fit their personal desires or needs. Being oblivious to the needs of those around them. In many countries, witches are exposed and punished. Even in the United States, in old Salem, women or men who practiced the art of witchcraft or manipulation were punished. Adultery and prostitution was just a form of witchcraft and those were identified with a scarlet letter. These ungodly actions destroy a society, destroy families destroy countries, destroy churches and need to be exposed.

Of course she was already of royalty and married into royalty again through Ahab. Others are voted in or appointed to and pay to get into high positions. Once the witch gets into a position of authority or power they are consistent and vigorous, in drafting, manipulating, conniving and pushing to gather like Jezebels around them. For some unknown reason they will all agree that men are inferior and they hate men. Unless the men are also witches. Evil loves to hang together. They will agree among themselves and that no matter what anyone says two plus two equal five. It's interesting that the Jezebel is brazen in her actions yet seems to get ahead. The Jezebel spirit is a very capable and convincing liar. That spirit is brazen and bullish. Jezebel's hatred of prophets (men of GOD was so fierce she even warned them she was going to kill them. Elijah, the prophet who had stood against the prophets of Belial, fled when he heard Jezebel had proclaimed his death. In modern times we see the effects of the Jezebel spirit when Pastors, Evangelist and other men of God are seduced by this spirit and are shamed by the fall. The seduction was planned, implemented and completed to the satisfaction of the Jezebels. Another victory by Jezebel.

The Bible warns of and end time church which allows the Jezebel spirit (calling herself a prophetess) to teach and seduce God's servants to commit fornication and worship idols. Rev. 2-20). "Notwithstanding I (the Lord) have a few things against thee because thou sufferest that woman Jezebel which calleth herself a prophetess to teach and to seduce my servants to commit fornication and to eat things sacrificed unto idols. And I gave her space to repent and she repented not behold I will cast her into a bed, and them that commit adultery with her into great tribulation except they repent of their deeds. I might interject once again that the adultery here is also taken as the spiritual adultery specifically that of worshiping Satan and or other gods. We see no examples of women being Pastors either in Old Testament or the New Testament. The Bibles says that a women is not to usurp authority over a man. Many secular churches now ordain woman Pastors. I can't judge the activity or the teachings. I neither watch them on TV nor attend the churches. There are times when attending a revival that a women who says she has been called to preach breaks into the service. It seems to me that it is most always out of vanity and trying to "stomp" on the evangelist message. It almost always starts out "they say a woman can't preach," etc. The movie star. Burt Lancaster, played a preacher called Elmer Gantry in a movie. It sounded like he was preaching. I guess anyone with enough practice could preach and teach. That doesn't mean God called them to the work.

Thankfully there are very few of the Jezebel types. You may or may not recognize this particular spirit immediately. They are capable of great deceit. The most obvious indicator is that she will have a hatred of God and Godly men. She will shun church completely. If she does attend her ulterior motive would be to somehow hinder or destroy the fundamental teachings of the church. Example is that she would try to find or point out reasons why abortion is allowed. The Jezebel will find excuses and even misread Bible scripture to allow homosexuals, child molesters and other lost men and women into the pulpit. She doubtfully will not have given anything or done any good for someone unless she reaps a tenfold reward. But again, the reward is the satisfaction she obtains from doing evil. It is more than a coincidence that the Jezebel spirit is responsible for Bibles being taken out of schools.

Bibles put in churches with only the New Testament and Psalms

The history and correction and reasoning cannot be made without the Old Testament. Bibles reprinted to leave out certain words. Only 66 canonized books allowed to circulate. Some denominational churches being reduced to social clubs Darwinism being accepted by schools as fact rather than theory. Planned Parenthood is just another scheme to kill and destroy and control. To make sacrifices to the dark side and to stop the spread of human dignity. The organization has spread across the globe as a woman's rights issue and has been partially funded by sacrificing baby parts to assist in experimentation of atheist and probably witch scientist. Unsuspecting men and women have also funded this organization through tax dollars. You get what you vote for. Witches are the coven that gathers together to scheme against any good done by the leaders of our land. Including our president and most certainly Israel. We will cover more of these evils later. The Jezebel spirit of witchcraft has all of the spirits we have listed in this book both prior to and in later chapters. Except possibly the spirit of fear. I have wondered for a long time about the ways we promote this evil in our midst. Every year we dress out little angels in witch uniforms and send them out to trick or treat. Is this a planned recruitment? Are the witch TV programs just tools to lead our young women into darkness? Does the Jezebel spirit influence the way the Hollywood crowd dresses and worships. Seems odd that when I mention it to even Christian women they will remark that it just harmless. I don't believe that. I think everything we do influences those young and innocent minds in the direction of good and evil. Again, this is the spirit that hates godly men, Pastors, and churches.

Bluff 9

Spirit of Revenge

Speaking of political situations, lets jump to an example the Bibles New Testament. It is another instance of a rather interesting situation that involved a King. King Herod was an ungodly man, who lived in the days of Jesus. Herod apparently had very few scruples. His queen, Herodius, was actually his brother's wife. I guess the fact that it was all in the family was justification enough for this queen to be in an adulteress relationship. To her the King was just another step up the power ladder Adultery at that time was not only frowned on but to the Israelite's, was punishable by stoning. The King and Queen were both aware of this but like all royalty felt they were above the common laws of God and men. Herodius, the queen brought with her into the relationship, her brazen and not to shy a daughter was named Salome. It was not a good example to set before the citizens.

John the Baptist was a prophet who Jesus himself called the greatest prophet that ever lived. He was also a dynamic preacher in that he called a sin a sin and pretty much didn't hold back on the truth. John made it his mission to point out the sins of men and to call them to repentance. John was loved, respected and feared among the people. Of course King Herod and his wife Herodius hated him. Herodius, the queen especially hated him because; well, he was a man of God and she was guilty of adultery. She tried everything imaginable to get Herod the King to kill him. We can imagine that it was every trick possible charm and manipulation she could think of. The nagging was pretty much constant. The King was wicked but no fool. He had put John the Baptist in prison as the result of her nagging. However, he knew the people loved John and they might revolt if he was slain. Killing John the Baptist was the only thing he had not done for her and she was furious.

The spirit of revenge does not give up. It is like a vulture which has to have the patience to wait for the prey to weaken. Herodius simply waited and we are certain did not miss an opportunity to bring the up the subject

King Herod was having a party. As usual his parties were a reason to invite the boys in and drink a little and have some royal fun. On that evening the adulteress wife Herodius formulated a plan as she saw the King weaken. She knew very well his weak points. He was already an adulterer and she had obviously noticed his attention to her daughter Salome. We sometimes hear the saying she knew exactly which buttons to push to get him to react her way. Salome must have been quite a looker. This spirit must be where a terrible mother of today get the idea to use the daughter as lures. To meet other men, or get drugs or whatever else is desirable. Maybe the spirit of Herodius. But not always to get revenge. Herodius dressed her daughter Salome in an alluring dance costume. No doubt it showed as much skin as was necessary to get an already weakened and drunk King to fall into lust. She sent Salome out to dance. The more he drunk the better she looked. Sound familiar to any of you? The old lust got hold of him and of course already being an adulterer and justifying that he was only a step father he made a pass at her. The idiot offered her up to half his kingdom and anything else she wanted. The party was going pretty strong at this point and the men partying with him heard his promise. As planned, and being the faithful daughter, and having followed the examples of her mother went to see her mother for direction. She said Mom the old fool has promised me anything. Now most mothers would have said tell the old fool to sober up and leave you alone. But the spirit of Herodius was so vengeful she prostituted her daughter. She told Salome tell him you want the head of John the Baptist. Like a lot of drunks and fools he had been trapped. He lusted after the little tramp that had so feverishly danced in front of him and he had to keep a promise witnessed by all of his peers. King Herod ordered the guards to behead the greatest prophet who ever lived. Soon they brought John the Baptist head in on a platter and gave it to the tramps Salome who in turn of course handed it over to the very delighted and triumphant adulteress queen. Just another mother who had experience in manipulation and obviously counted on the desire weakness of men. She chose to pass all that knowledge on to her daughter. Her guidance brought her own daughter to damnation by her evil lust for power and revenge.

We wonder how many mothers of today are setting the correct example for the daughters. Unfortunately some mothers try to act like their sisters and dress more like teenagers. Not unusual to see a mother and daughter both dressed in miniskirts and flirting with the young men. They appear to be very flirtatious and or promiscuous.

Back in the day we had other adjectives we used to describe them. A few were called skags, split tails, easys, sluts, and a few not to be written. Also back in the day, good mothers would advise the sons that it was best to see what the mother is like because the nut doesn't fall far from the tree. Herodius and Salome are good examples. Dads would say to their sons "don't date a girl you wouldn't marry". Another wise input from dad was like mother like daughter. That's what she will look like and be when she gets older. If she bosses her poor husband around be careful.

The Herodius spirit is observed when we see various scenes set up by mothers who try to stay young by being best friends with the daughter and the daughter's friends. In the news we hear of the daughters being prostituted to get street drugs. It is obvious that even Godly men can be led down the primrose path by the wiles and temptations of evil women. Of course the fact that an evil woman made herself available to him because she wanted something, and practically forced herself on him, and made certain she showed him a lot of skin, and caught him in a weakened state, in today's world means it's still the man's fault and he should have resisted and simply run away from the situation. Actually that is good advice and just what he should do. Run like the devil was after him. It's hard to sometimes see the trap. A lonely man is easy prey.

With all the exposure to sexual innuendo, we see in commercials in prime time it's no wonder the world is getting brainwashed to violence and promiscuity. It's no wonder so many children including both boys and girls are being kidnapped and sold into slavery. First of all let's get it straight; there is absolutely no justification for the sexual perversion we see in the world today. The perversion with children should be high on the list to prosecute and stop completely. Punishment should be that so strict that even the weirdest pervert would hesitate, if not stop in its track at even the thought of child molesting. That includes the so called men of the cloth whose perversion has been going on long enough. The drug situation has addled the mind of both men and women to the point that sex with anyone or anything is permitted and condoned. Some adults haven't got enough sense to realize that children are children. Especially when we see mothers sending there little girls out in miniskirts and dolled up like they were adults. What is to be accomplished by this other than to expose them to perverts and rapist? There is no justification for any of the sexual misconduct we see going on but I think we would see much less of it if women would wear less seductive clothing. You're going to catch whatever bait you use. I know, I know, you should have the freedom be able to wear whatever you want without someone bothering you. "Grow up", Be responsible. Be reasonable. We see in the news and read constantly of children being put on the market for the purpose of obtaining drugs. Its only speculation but she probably should never have become a mother. In today's world a girl needs her mother to be a mother. Probably more so than any other time in history. She needs to trust and learn and be protected by her mother.

Getting back to the Herodius spirit. It is obviously evil and as a result hates to come under conviction of wrong doing. Rarely will we see this spirit in a church where truth is taught. If she does go to church it is most likely in rebellion to godliness. Most likely it is all about appearances most likely it will be in a secular church where sin is not condemned. It is haughty, self-serving, selfish and unloving. It may be dressed in fine lines and bright colors but underneath all the trappings is a black heart.

Bluff 10

Spirit of entrapment xxx

The spirit of entrapment is the fastest growing damning spirit today. One of the wisest men who ever lived wrote this little article.

Proverbs 7, Say unto wisdom, thou art my sister, and call understanding thy kinsman: that thou may keep thee from the strange woman, from the stranger that which is flattered by her words. For at the window of my house I looked through my casement and beheld among the simple ones, I discerned a youth, a young man void of understanding, passing through the street near her corner and he went the way into her house. In the twilight, in the evening in the black and dark night. And behold there met him a woman with the attire of a harlot and subtle of heart. She is loud and stubborn: her feet abide not in her house. Now is she without, now in the streets, and lieth in wait at every corner. So she caught him and kissed him and with an impudent face said unto him. I have peace offerings with me; this day have I paid my vows. Therefore came I forth to meet thee, diligently to seek thy face and I have found thee. I have decked my bed with coverings of tapestry, with carved works, with fine linen of Egypt. I have perfumed my bed with myrrh, aloes and cinnamon. Come let us take our full of love until the morning: let us solace ourselves with love. For the Goodman is not at home, he is gone a long journey. He hath taken a bag of money with him and will come home at the day appointed. With her much fair speech she caused him to yield, with the flattering of her lips she forced him. He goeth after her straight way as an ox goeth to slaughter or as a fool to the correction of the stocks. Till a dart strike through his liver; as a bird hasteneth to the snare and knoweth not it is for his life. Hearken unto me now therefore all ye children and attend to the words of my mouth. Let not thine heart decline to her ways, go not astray in her paths. For she has cast down many wounded yea many strong men have been slain by her. Her house is the way to hell going down to the chamber of death.

The spirit of entrapment also links with and creates many problems in our world today. It' is true that many strong and important men have been slain and will be shamed by this spirit. Some accusations are true. Many accusations are false or exaggerated. Many important men's positions and reputation are being slain by this spirit. A promise or hint of sex in payment for favors or position is a spirit that is being played and capitalized on by a small percentage of women all over America. There whoredoms are mostly to gain positions of authority, to be notice, to minimize their own guilt in the adulteress act or as the scorned woman who did not get the part or position to take revenge. Perhaps, just to be the woman who gets her ten minutes of fame, and gains notoriety by bringing famous men down. The present movement is positive proof that where there is great freedom sadly is great promiscuity. The USA is not regarded as a moral nation because of the pornography, and sexual immorality that is displayed by our constant divorcing and remarrying and promiscuity. Living together without marriage is simply an admission on both parts that it is for convenience only, and both are simply waiting for someone richer or better looking to come around. Some fool probably will.

The spirit of entrapment applies to many of the relationships that is created by at least one of the parties not wanting to be trapped into bondage as the result of sexual favors. The spirit again is all about control. Generally, the actions of a cougar is observed. A "Cougar" is the name given to an older woman who stalks or preys on men or boys, much younger. The high school teacher who secretly dates one of her students is a good example. Relationships with men of her own age has not been successful and she preys on the young men to fulfill her lust and the need to control the situation. If you have ever noticed a fat, middle aged teacher trying to charm the boys in her room it is almost hilarious. Many of these woman have a serious problem with reality. Just about anywhere a woman has control over a much younger group of children they consider themselves intellectually and physically superior to the point of becoming goddesses. I once knew a woman who being rather obese would walked around on her tip toes to make herself appear lighter.

The spirit of entrapment explains itself. Trapped with someone you really don't like. Trapped in a situation you can't get out of. The bait used to trap a man is sexual. Trapped by a lying, crying tear jerker, woman who knows exactly what buttons to push to control you. The only solution is to walk as far away from it as you can and fight and win the temptation not to return to the trap. Don't worry about her. She will find another victim before you are out of sight.

Many of the older civilizations have experienced these difficulties and overcome them with certain rules.

The Muslims community with its ancient wisdom requires that both men and women dress modestly and not display or expose anything that would attempt to seduce a man. The Indian culture dresses modestly for the same reason. Several religious groups require the women to dress modestly. The Amish and Mennonites as well as other denominations that flourish in America frown on exposing body parts that entice lust. It is interesting to note that while in many cultures the parents arrange the marriage that those are the marriages that last and are happy. Ancient wisdom has taught these cultures reality.

Personality, faithfulness and partnership in raising another generation of loving, caring, god fearing children should be high on the priority list.

The Woodstock era of the 1960 was a disaster for the morality of a younger generation when the pied piper of sexual freedom led so much of Americas youth into the trap of get it all now it's free. Do anything you want no one cares and it will not hurt you. A terrible trap that we hope history has taught us never to let it happen again. Only parents can stop it. Parents who join it should be punished. They will be. You reap what you sow. The trap stands at the doorway and beckons us to come in. It will not hurt you. Come in it is free. Most assuredly as history teaches us it will be a woman who leads the man into the trap. We see this trap being laid for meek men especially.

Men do need and yearn for a helpmate. A hindermate is a trap that will ruin his life.

The spirit of entrapment does not always use skin, perfume, beauty, and seduction to draw men into the trap. Probably one of the most harming fairytales ever written was the story of Cinderella. The poor little stepsister who always had to do all the work. The one in the family who was the less favored. Dad and mom always loved everyone else best. She had to do all the cooking and wash the dishes and ironing and everyone else just sat around doing nothing. Poor little Cinderella. Until you're in the trap. Finding out she doesn't cook, clean, iron, keep house or anything else except to wear the glass slipper. All that other work reminds her to much of how bad she was treated. It makes her sad. If she can find anyone to do it for her she will. Otherwise it probably won't be done. She will tell her sad story to someone else and the nice person will feel sorry for her and do it for her. Sooner or later she finds the story works so well and she is too sad to do anything so everyone does everything for Cinderella. Sure sure. Get out of the trap.

To those male readers, the Wisdom of Solomon gives a little advice in Proverbs 31- 10 about finding a virtuous women. Maybe that will get you into the Bible. I hope so. The Proverbs are the greatest wisdom you will ever read with exception of the words of Jesus.

Bluff 11

Spirit of confusion

One of the extreme examples in the scriptures of the spirit of confusion is in Genesis 19. The city of Sodom was inhabited by and taken over by homosexuals. A man called Lot lived in the city along with his wife and two daughters. God was going to destroy the city but found that Lot was a righteous man and told him to take his family and get out. Lot of course obeyed and took his family out of the city.

As his family left the city Lot's wife looked back. Apparently, she was confused, and either liked or condoned the immoral practice of the inhabitants. God turned her into a pillar of salt. Modern archaeologist have found this city and agree that it was burned confirming the Scriptures. Whether you believe the story or not, historical evidence pretty much substantiate that it is true. His daughters later rebelled against God's laws. Here the spirit of justification fits the reason for their fornication and incest. Living in the filth of the city had somewhat brainwashed them into justifying that it was acceptable. Confused. The Scriptures give us an example of someone who may have escaped the immorality personally but somehow condones the activity and even desires to be around it. God completely destroyed the city.

We often ask ourselves why would a loving God completely destroy the city?. After reading of the destruction of not only some of the cities and inhabitants, it appears he cleansed them with fire. And burned, most of them along with the animals. I think we have to come to the conclusion, right or wrong, that these cities were so infested with diseases such as aids or syphilis that it was the only way to cleanse the world and keep the righteous people from contacting the plaques. God also destroyed the animals possibly due to the bestiality, or sex with animals, that was occurring. This habit was also condemned by God.

Concerning the children. They are innocent in God's eyes. God loves children. The parents had either transmitted the disease or the children were in danger of being molested by the diseased people. God will take care of the children and they are much better of with God than in the world they were being exposed to. Think how we as parents would feel if our innocent children were savagely molested by a diseased group of people. Some diseases like aids will be carried by them all their lives. Is it no wonder that we caution strongly against this confusion of the sexes and morality that has spread across our world.

The parents of the children in this city and other heathen cities were probably worshiping a God call BAAL. They believed that sacrificing the children helped them gain wealth. I think they sometimes just had babies and let them die of whatever reason was convenient. WE hear stories in the news that women have discarded the newborns in restrooms, garbage bags and dumpsters. Some have sacrificed their babies or young children, both male and female to drug dealers and pimps. When we condone homosexuality and bestiality and promiscuity in the form of political correctness we have told our children that it's and OK and a choice of lifestyle;. What God are you serving? It has to stop.

New Testament scriptures try to tell us how to get away from this confusion. I don't believe that people are born homosexual. I do believe that they can become confused as to their sexuality. The responsibility lies with the parents. Parents need to be a male father and a female mother. Other combinations do not work. I don't agree with abortion at all. The answer JUST SAY NO. We should hate that our children are molested by this out of control confused spirit. That includes, a small percent. The Clergy that has somehow lost control.

This spirit is obvious and easy to discern. When the scriptures write about battles in high places we can use it to realize that its possibly pointing to the battles we have in our minds concerning the information, or lack of information we gather on these subjects. Again. History teaches us and the scriptures reveal wisdom.

Romans 1-22, Professing themselves wise, they became fools. And the glory of the incorruptible God into an image made like to corruptible man and to birds and to four footed beast and creeping things. Wherefore God gave them up to uncleanliness through the lust of their own hearts to dishonor their own bodies between themselves: Who changed the truth of God into a lie and worshipped and served the creature more than the Creator who is blessed forever, AMEN

For this cause God gave them over to vile affections: for even their women did change the natural use into that which is against nature. And likewise also the men leaving the natural use of the woman, burned in their lust one toward another, men with men working that which is unseemly, and receiving in themselves that recompense of their error which was meet. And even as they did not to retain God in their knowledge, God gave them over to a reprobate mind to do those things which are not convenient.

The word reprobate means that there is no discernment between what is good and what is bad. A bad situation that only gets worse. Sadly to say, and, I do feel sorry for that trapped spirit,. It eventually leads to destruction. It is not a lifestyle that is easily pulled away from. It is a trap and a snare that should not be entered into. It is a chosen destiny. Sadly, I know men and women who have fallen into the trap.

2 Timothy 3-16. All scripture is given by inspiration of God and is profitable for doctrine, for reproof, for correction, for instruction in righteousness. That the man of God may be perfect, thoroughly furnished unto all good works.

Scriptures tell us that ungodly men & women who will be trying to lead us into the trap will call these fables and will tell us only those things we wants to hear and or sugar coat the terrors that come from disobedience.

Some things matter a lot and some things may seem trivial but make a big testimony. We don't have to carry signs, and picket or have rallies to make a difference. Just let people be aware that your silence on the matter does not mean that you condone it. When they turn to me and say "right"? I'm' likely to say "not right" if I disagree.

God is not the author of confusion. Confused minds can be set straight with scriptures. Yes, the Scriptures do say that men and women should dress differently and not try to look like the opposite sex.

1st Corinthians 11, if a man has long hair it is a shame to him. If a woman has long hair it is a glory to her. This scripture is taken seriously in many religions that want to seriously separate themselves from a generation that is losing track of their birth gender.

1st Timothy 2:9, Women should adorn themselves in modest apparel with shamefacedness and sobriety.

In the Book of Leviticus, the laws of Gods are established. I know, I know some are yelling legalist. But, the laws of God will never change and even Paul said the law is good if used lawfully. I am using it lawfully to explain what god likes and doesn't like. Sexual morality s pointed out in Leviticus 18; Incest is forbidden.

Verse 22 says "Thou shall not lie with mankind as with womankind. It is an abomination. Neither shall thou lie with any beast to defile thyself therewith, neither shall a woman stand before a beast to lie down thereof: it is confusion.

Verse 29, do not prostitute thy daughter to cause her to be a whore.

Leviticus 20. Penalties of disobedience. Time for the reader to get involved.

Confusion is the state of being in question about any one thing or several things. Confusion can be brought about in the young minds by an admired sports figure or a movie star who themselves are caught in the trap. Misery does like company and birds of feather do flock together. This book is intended to show the bait hat is in the trap. It's up to you to avoid it if you want to live a successful and happy life.

Bluff 12

Despair

There have been periods in history where morality abounds and the faith is that things will get better. King Solomon was a man greatly blessed by God with a supernatural wisdom. Men and women came from afar to seek his wisdom on many subjects. The queen of Sheba visited him as a result of his reputation. She was so impressed that she sent great treasures to express her admiration.

King Solomon had many wives as a result of political relationships. They were political marriages. It was common for a king to marry the daughter of the King or ruler of another country to establish peaceful relationships.

Solomon's many alien wives created a lot of problems. Being from other countries they brought in different Gods' and religions. They wanted to build temples to these heathen gods. Some of these gods required prostitution and even got to the point of baby sacrifices. Solomon wrote in proverbs:

Proverbs 21-19. It is better to dwell in the wilderness than with a contentious and angry woman. Proverbs 27 15. A continual dropping in a very rainy day and a contentious woman are alike.

We could go on about these Proverbs but part of the reason for this book is to get the reader interested in the Bible. I personally don't understand why Proverbs are mot taught in schools. Or maybe I do.

Obviously it was beginning to tire this great King having to deal with the many varieties of religions, needs, traditions etc of these wives.

We can search out his despair when he wrote in Ecclesiastes 7

"And I find more bitter than death the woman whose heart is snares and nets, and her hands as bands; whoso pleaseth God shall escape from her, but the sinner shall be taken by her. Behold this I have found saith the preacher counting one by one, to find out the account ;: which yet my soul seeketh, but I find not; One man among a thousand have I found, but a woman among these I have not found. Lo this only have I found that God hath made man upright but they have sought out many inventions.

Apparently Solomon was running with the wrong crown at the time and being politically correct was the wrong direction to go. At that time there were many women that would have made him happy and he probably would have had many children.

Bluff 13

Familiar Spirits

There is hope. We read of a women called Mary from a town called Magdela that was processed by seven spirits. She is referred to as Mary Magdeline. It is likely that if a woman displays the characteristics of any of the other spirits mentioned that she has underlying spirits as well. As such we can usually find attached to many if not all the problems we face in society as having a spiritual root. Just naming a few of these problem lets us take a look around us and observe society in its darkest form.

We can easily observe Fear, Drunkenness, Tardiness, Meddling, Gossiping, Lying, Addiction, Division, Rage, Jealousy, Scoffing, Greed, Sloppiness, Stealing, Manipulation, unloving, and bitterness. We probably could add a few more.

These are commonly referred to as "familiar spirits". Why are they called familiar? Because much of the time they are handed down from generation to generation. And found common in households. We therefore get the phrases "like mother like daughter and "the apple doesn't fall far from the tree. Without a doubt, analysis of family should be an important part of picking out a lifetime partner for either gender. They are also called familiar because they are so evident and numerous that we get used to them and for the most part tolerate them. Some call them bad habits. They can be much more damaging.

At one time some of these sayings were disregarded and counted as old wives tales and foolishness. Now with the new scientific findings regarding DNA we can prove that many traits both good and bad can be inherited. Genetically it becomes fact rather than fiction.

How do these spirits affect others? For example: The spirit of tardiness is connected to the spirit of manipulation which is the desire to control the time of others. The matriarchal spirit is observed in the female domineering her household. Most assuredly creating confusion and division in a family where men are present. Control generally being gained by much verbal manipulation. If there is a matriarchal society whether present or ancient which has flourished and survived please let me know. I have not found any evidence of it.

The Society is affected. Dictionary definition of society: The system of community life in which individuals form a continuous and regulatory association for their mutual benefit and protection. All of the above listed, spiritual traits, effect society in a negative way.

The family is affected. Dictionary definition of family: Parents and their children. Parent defined of course as male and female of the human species

Is it possible that these spirits can come from sources other than inheritance? The internet is a common source for information. For example, a succubus is a female demon who draws men into a sexual relationship in order to steal their soul. In attempting to do research on the subject I went to the best source being the internet now I know why they call it the web. Like a spiders web it can be a trap. I didn't go very far into the search till it became apparent that this was as a source being used by evil to create evil. I stopped the search. Curious, after a period of time, I tried again to get a better idea of the Jewish folklore.

I stopped again. It is a channel being used by evil to bring people to a passive state concerning evil. Much like pornography and the quigi board. I suggest staying away from any web page or game that brings witchcraft or demonology into focus. Very dangerous. It is nothing more than door to open demonic spirits. Very easy to enter in but almost impossible to get rid off.

Some believe they can be gotten through dealing with fortune tellers, astrologers, and Quigi boards, pornography, witchcraft, idols and mostly recently in our own generation the television and internet. Television is brainwashing both men and women of today.

Every program is meant to somehow ridicule men and make women look superior. The advertisement are even geared toward the emasculation of men. Emasculation defined as taking every approach to turn men in wimps or to emasculate them. It's working. Men are much more effeminate than they were 30 years ago. Woman are much more masculine (sadly) than they were 30 years ago.

Up until puberty, boys usually have a few feminine traits. Hormones still working overtime to keep up with physical growth. Exposure to other men and especially the father soon puts the boy in right direction to become masculine in thought and physically. Without this exposure feminine traits may linger for quite a while. Girls also display some male traits. Again exposure and contact with to the mother soon brings out the feminine side. Without the exposure of both parents there may be a confusion in the thought process which hampers the dominant birth gender. Thus we have a lot of tomboys and mama's boys around for a while.

Our cruel and ignorant society would immediately tag them homosexual and/or transsexual, and most likely for whatever ungodly reason try to force it on them. If a boy happens to be late in puberty he is found a slot where he can fit as being gay. He might even start believing it if his parents don't step into the situation and explain it. Of course a lot of "modern" parents might love all the attention it gets them from having a different child. The same situation occurs if the boy is not athletic or the girl is a not beauty queen. Remember they inherited from the parent. If the sexual organs are male they are male. If the sexual organs are female, they are female. They should be listed, recorded, trained as and guided through their childhood to be the person they were born to be. Any intrusion or manipulation creates confusion, sickness unhappiness and many times a suicidal tendency in these young men and women.

Boys are being turned effeminate by many teachers who, rather than realize they are showing masculine traits will diagnose a condition whereas medicine is necessary to calm them down. Boys will be boys. Of course medicating the child is an advantage to the teacher and sometimes the parent even though it is harmful to the child. It is a better way that the boy be reprimanded and even paddled. Sorry mother. If paddled, your son might grow up to be a man and not a wimp. A paddling is a badge of honor to most young men. To others that observe it a reason to behave. To most young girls he will be brave and be held in high esteem as a boy and not transgender, or a wimp and most likely not gay. It seems girls of all ages like bad boys. I think this method of correction is approved by the timeless wisdom of spare the rod and spoil the child. A lot cheaper and much more efficient than medication. It will be discovered by modern man that it is a whole lot safer. Of course the ancient wisdom knew this already. I still recall the saying: Little girls are made of sugar and spice and everything nice and little boys are made of snails, nails and puppy dog tails. YUP

Bluff 14

A Solution: X

We have to admit that things are going in the wrong direction. People are not happy unless they are either high on drugs or alcohol. These are short term fixes only to be followed by regrets and loss of valuable time. Time, which could have been spent in analyzing the truth and the lies that confronts us daily.

Women have an edge on men only in the ability to put into words constantly how they feel, what they want and what they don't want. They can speak constantly about trivia, change the subject if they find it necessary to keep control of the conversation and if necessary revert to tears at the snap of a finger. Women have the ability to make men think that it was the woman's idea from the beginning.

I am sure that men and women have a different thought process. Men get to the conclusion much faster and automatically sort out the trivia that would keep them from reaching a goal or conclusion. It is a thought process they have adapted to for the sake of survival of both the species. It may not seem at first to be the best but will save time and work itself out The thought process put simply is, (2+2=4), two plus two equal four, Women on the other hand think 2+3-1=4 (two plus three minus one equal four). Usually reaching the same correct conclusion by a different approach. This is probably a good thing if used constructively and may avoid some pitfalls or problems along the way to the conclusion getting them out in the open and thus avoiding problems later on. It also can create a lot of arguments and unhappiness. This is especially true in child raising and financial decisions. Married couples need more than anything to understand that the two thinking processes assure greater success and happiness in life. A nagging and contentious wife and a stubborn husband will be doomed to unhappiness.

If we elected only men to our political leadership we would be much better off. All women would be represented by this group of men. Because it is obvious that they have chosen good helpmates. I am positive the Senator or Congressman would be influenced in a positive way by his wife. Behind every good man is a good wife.

On the other hand, and it is quite obvious, that a contentious woman, having racial issues who may be of a minority group and can't get out of the 2+3=4 stage is going to create division and problems. Progress is the last thing on her mind. Only her personal Jezebel agenda is important to her. Our voting public needs to consider that the person they are voting into office should truly represent them. It is terrible that we have to sometimes choose between two obviously unqualified people. Perhaps we need more decent, good people running for office. Kind of like a lamb going in with the tigers. I'll vote for the lamb

Women have to have men to function efficiently. Men only need women for purposes of childbearing. Since men need women if they want to have children, the choice of a woman for purpose of happiness is an essential decision the young man has to make if he is going to have a happy and fruitful life. Everything mentioned so far in this book should be taken into consideration in picking a helpmate.

Realist would admit that we have gone too far in the wrong direction. Being a romantic and looking through a glass darkly I believe that it's time for men to take a stand and to take back the authority that is there birthright. First, I believe that a man needs to choose a wife that is going to be loyal and faithful. A woman who displays any of the spirit traits discussed can make a man's life miserable. He will find himself handing over his paycheck, allowed only trivial decisions, if any, and without realizing it be the joke of the town because she is running around with everything in pants.

You can't judge a woman on her looks. There are beautiful tramps and ugly tramps. All out to trap a man into marriage. The old saying I chased her till she caught me is true. The best thing that has happened to men in the last hundred years is the DNA test. It absolutely identifies the father of the child. All the weeping and promising and begging in the world would not get me to marry one of the modern day women without a DNA test proving it was mine. The few Maury TV shows that I watched by accident has got me convinced. Some of the women don't even know who the father could be. Could have been any of maybe five. You have to wonder what was on these people's minds. Also you hope that whatever is on their minds is not contagious. I think the next best thing that could happen is a pill that takes a man's mind off women until he decides it's time to settle down and start a family. A pill that lets him think clearly without all the sexuality, seduction, manipulation taking place to get him to bite the apple.

Taking a stand doesn't mean the kind of ME TO silliness that is going to backfire. In retrospect it's a good thing that men see the spitefulness and entrapment that is behind the movement. Women use sexuality constantly to get men's attention, then when they get the attention cry they were misunderstood, abused, raped, drugged or whatever excuse they can use to rid themselves of the guilt of whoredom or to crucify another good man. It's time to ignore the flirting's and games and for men to get on about building a life for themselves. Once a man has been alone long enough to realize what they want without a women telling them what they want they will be much happier in life. The man should pick out the helpmate that fits into his lifestyle. Not pick a hinder mate who wants to change him. It's good to have a wife, a companion and a help mate in life. But many of the women with the spirits defined will be a definite hinder mate. It is good to have a family. The best family will be the one where the man is the head of the house.

Have you also noticed that most of the TV programs and commercials depict the male as stupid, or inferior to the female? I think it is time to boycott these TV programs. Certainly, it's time to stop buying the products that they advertise. About a year of not buying the products would halt some of the nonsense. We should stop hiring women just because they are women. If a female can do the job better then obviously the smart thing for management to do is hire her. But usually what happens is the female ends up with a cushy job while the men get the dirty grunt jobs. Of course equal pay is expected. Women have wormed there way into positions in government where they have the authority to hire. When they hire for the cushy jobs its always other women

Now women want to show their superiority by being referees at soccer and football games. Good thing if you have that spirit of hate and want to control men.

I think if we all would take a sincere and honest look at what is going on around us we would be very concerned about a world dominated by this one or two percent of the women we have described. The spirit of Jezebel for example in control would result in a confused, chaotic and deadly society without morals. That society will not last. We may have one generation to fix the problem.

The minority and manipulators and witches would draw our attention to global warming, save the whales, gun control, endangered species, women's rights, gay rights, etc. Minority meaning the one percent of our global population who want to tell everyone else what to do because they don't fit it with the honorable, good decent people who are striving to make things better. They cry freedom of speech while damning everything that is said in truth and honesty by those who disagree with them.

The solution is one that is found in our Bibles. John 3 says that a person must be born again. Born of the spirit. Whatever bad spirit that has come upon people through society, exposure to evil, miss information or even at birth can be rebuked by accepting Jesus Christ as savior. By accepting him and his spirit your sins will be forgiven and you can come into a new knowledge. I suggest you run to the nearest Christian church and listen intently to what the Pastor tells you. It doesn't matter what the name over the door is or the color of the people inside. As long as it a Christian church adhering to the words of Jesus. There is only one God, there is only one Son, and there is only one Holy spirit. Read the Bible. Read those things that were written here so you can get confirmation of the truth. The Bible calls it being brought from darkness to light. An ungodly society, where men and women will live in terror is on its way if we don't start caring for humans more than we do animals.

Bluff 15

Conclusion

Physical violence has never solved anything. It is indeed the tool of the devil and the world. All of the accusations, yelling and screaming and threats we see coming from the world is never going to solve the problem. Accusations only serve to feed the accusers spirit. Sometimes it seems the spirits have to be fed even if the situation doesn't require it.

We claim Christianity in the United States and are the center for the Evangelism that spreads the gospel. The scriptures have a lot of advice in having a happy marriage. All authority is given by God. It is God who puts people in power and we have seen in world history, godly rulers as well as ungodly rulers. We also have seen how God used both to bring about his end plan. The goal is established and will come to pass. Prophecy will be fulfilled.

The Bible tells us that God is the head. 1 Corinthians 11-3 "But I would have you know, that the head of every man is Christ; and the head of every woman is the man: and the head of Christ is God. The man has authority over the woman in the marriage. Notice children aren't mentioned. That means they have no authority. It's about time the head of the house took responsibility for the family. That does not mean dictatorship. Even if he delegates the decision to his wife he is still responsible in the eyes of God.

The media would have us to believe that the children are wiser than the parents when it comes to making decisions. Of course the parents know better. Or do they? Seem like a lot of brats are running the household.

Couples living together of course are not under this authority. They are in adultery and have already rejected the sanctified relationship God intended.

1 Corinthians 6. He who is joined to a harlot is one body

1 Timothy 2. Confirms the instructions for Godly women. "In like manner also that that women adorn themselves in modest apparel with shamefacedness and

sobriety; not with broided hair, or gold, or pearls, or costly array; But (which becometh women professing godliness) with good works. Let the woman learn in silence with all subjection but I suffer not a woman to teach, nor to usurp authority over the man, but to be in silence. Reasoning again to explain a little of this is that women and men do not think the same way. Has nothing to do with intelligence.

1 Timothy 5. Instructions for widows; Available in the Bible if you care to read it. If you are a widow this book will help you more that any self-help book on the market.

Probably one of the most important scriptures pertaining to women whether married or single is in 2 Timothy 3-6 and concerns a very up to date scenario about people being led astray;

This also know that in the last days perilous times will come. For men shall be lovers of their own selves, covetous, boasters, proud, blasphemers, disobedient to parents, thankful, unholy. Without natural affection, truce-breakers, false accusers, incontinent, fierce, despisers of those that are good. Traitors, heady, high minded, lovers of pleasures more than lovers of God.

Having a form of godliness, but denying the power there of from such turn away.

For of this sort are they which creep into houses, and lead captive silly women laden with sins, led away with divers lust, Ever learning and never able to come to the knowledge of the truth

We are indeed in perilous time. The ungodly news, TV sitcom, and spiritual leaders creep into houses and try to convince us through shame, repetition or whatever brainwashing techniques they can use that promiscuity, adultery, manipulation and all other sins are okay. They will convince both women and children, if possible, that the husband is an oaf, and a bungling fool. Because they want to destroy households.

The women need to be strong and of a godly spirit to overcome this plague of brainwashing and manipulation. Many of the women who are on TV promoting the various agendas have the Eve or want to be worshiped spirit

The men of the household have to be more aware of the spirits that are trying to take control of the family. That is one of the purposes of the book. As stated, previously, only a few women entertain and or are possessed by these spirits. But they are clamorous enough and loud enough and famous enough to create an ungodly and rebellious atmosphere in the home.

Men will have to rebel against the evil against the evil that is taking over our country. It should be a silent rebellion. A silent war that the enemy doesn't realize is taking place. Until you have won the battle.

Probably the most important is to get into a God fearing church that puts Jesus Christ at the head of its teachings. By doing this you expose your family to the truth. It is a time of family union and togetherness. You will meet others who are seeking or have already learned the truth.

Check over the scriptures in this book. You should always double check written works to see if they are consistent with God's word.

Note those companies who continue to downgrade men in their advertising. The agenda should be to sell a product based on it quality and price rather than to make the woman and children look smarter than the man by purchasing it.

Stop buying the products they advertise on TV shows and sitcoms that dwell on selling the women a product that the male would normally have a say, if not the decision to buy.

If your girlfriend want to see something or go somewhere that promotes only women's agenda let her go by herself or have her pay for it.

By the way if the girlfriend has to pay for food once in a while you will learn whether or not she really cares.

Stop hiring women just because they nag about equality. If they are better than the man or you need those in a certain position ok. I find it hard to believe that construction jobs need woman as flagmen because they are better at it.

If the music downgrades men don't buy it.

Stop voting for unqualified women. Your wife or girlfriend doesn't know how you vote.

If you're a man and married, the best thing you can do is love your wife and family and give them the attention they crave and deserve. We reap what we sow.

If you're a woman and married take head to those spirits that are out there that want to destroy you and your family. Most of all, be loyal and faithful. A man can hold his head high under all adverse condition if his wife stands by his side and is faithful only to him and God.

If you're still a single man. Read this book carefully. If you are looking for a helpmate start evaluating possibilities based on what's contained. You're never going to find a suitable loyal wife, dancing on the tables at a bar. More than likely the woman which will make you a good wife will be attending a church somewhere.

If nothing else I hope this effort will help solve a few problems. I am sure it will get a few people into reading the Bible

God Bless

Printed in the United States
By Bookmasters